BOOK 3

Setting Sail for the 4th Quarter of Life

Setting Sail for Retirement

Setting Sail for Estate Issues

Setting Sail for Living Trusts

Glossary

SETTING SAIL FOR THE 4TH QUARTER OF LIFE

First edition. September 7, 2023.

ISBN: 979-8232203979

Written by Sharon O'Maley.

Royal Tech Writers & Translators and the editors who have been involved with the production of this manual have produced this book as an educational tool for individuals or professionals in the most accurate and current manner possible. It is not written, however, for the purpose of giving legal advice to the reader or sold to render legal, accounting or any other professional service.

Information may change over a period of time, so RTW&T disclaim responsibility for any omission or inaccuracies in this particular text. RTW&T, consequently, does not accept liability for any actual or perceived loss resulting from the information in this book.

Chapter 1

Setting Sail For Retirement

COUNTDOWN TO RETIREMENT

The baby boomer generation is graying. More and more people are approaching retirement age. With Social Security's assets being consumed and the number of workers that will support it shrinking, we will have to rely more on our personal savings when it's time to retire. Over the years, a variety of options have been created to help Americans prepare for their golden years, including Annuities.

Approaching retirement, one will be faced with several key decisions, and making the right choices is crucial to a family's future. First of all, one needs to decide when to retire. Technically, that refers to when he or she starts receiving income from a retirement plan and Social Security. But once an individual starts receiving income from Social Security, the pension, the annuity, the IRA, or any other tax-deferred retirement plan, a chain of events will be triggered.

The first milestone is age 59 ½. Before that age, one cannot withdraw money from a retirement plan without incurring a penalty from the IRS. The next age milestone is sixty-two. At this point, one may start receiving Social Security benefits. Generally, it is advisable to wait until one reaches the age sixty-five because one forfeits 20% of Social Security retirement benefits. If the life expectancy numbers continue to rise, the loss could be substantial.

As for personal retirement plans, including pensions, IRAs, Keoghs, etc., it is recommended to let money continue to grow tax deferred for as long as possible. Now that the issue has been clarified as to when to start taking money out of retirement plans, an individual can look at what money to take out.

When an individual retires from a company, the 401 (k), 403 (b), or profit-sharing plan money may be distributed to one in a lump sum. If an individual decides to roll the money over into an IRA, he or she should not touch the money, or else the IRS will withhold 20%. A 401 (k) may be "income averaged" for tax purposes and an IRA may not.

Retirement Planning Techniques

MOST EXPERTS AGREE that an individual will need 75% or 80% of pre-retirement income to maintain the same standard of living before retiring. The question may be, "Why does someone need less than 100%?" An individual's expenses and taxes will probably go down in retirement. Inflation will almost certainly reduce the value of a dollar between now and when an individual retires, meaning that a $50,000 income ten or fifteen years from now will not buy as much as a $50,000 income today.

If an individual is planning to retire in five years and the annual rate of inflation during those years is 6% and the annual income today is $50,000. what will an individual need five years from now to match that amount at a 6% annual inflation rate? Take $50,000 and multiply it by the appropriate inflation multiplier from an Inflation Multiplier Chart. $50,000 x 1.34 = $67,000. Now that can be multiplied by 75% and that will give $50,250.

With that idea of how much annual income is needed in retirement, one must multiply that amount by the number of years till retirement. Men are now living to an average age of 72, and women are living to age 77. The further one is from retirement, the more likely it is that he or she will exceed these averages.

Annuities

An annuity is a contract between an individual and an insurance company. The very first annuities had guarantees of principal and a set rate of return offered by the issuing insurance company. That worked for a time, but lackluster rates of return prompted some annuity owners to push for more investment control.

The popularity of annuities, especially variable annuities, has exploded. Annuities have been very popular over the years because, by law, they are tax-deferred; money deposited grows annually without income taxes taken out each year.

Annuities come in two main types: Fixed and Variable. If an investor is a conservative investor looking for a consistent way to build a retirement savings, then fixed annuities may be the answer. However, if this individual is financially savvy and believes he or she can do better choosing his or her own investments, variable annuities offer much greater flexibility and control. As long as the money contributed to the annuity is destined to be used only at retirement, annuities can make a significant impact in the growth of a nest egg.

When one wishes to withdraw money, he or she has a variety of payment options to choose from. The insurance company can pay either in a lump sum, make periodic payments, or guarantee a lifetime of income on a tax-advantaged basis. All annuities, fixed or variable, share several common benefits:

Ideal for Estate Planning

Proceeds from annuities pass directly to beneficiaries without the delay, expense, and publicity of probate. This is a great advantage when an estate is going through a time-consuming legal process.

The Power of Tax Deferral

Because taxes are not paid on earnings every year, annuities enjoy "tax-deferral." Money inside an annuity earns interest on principal and interest. While an individual will have to pay taxes at some point, he or she is getting temporary use of the government's money, and it's earning interest.

No Contribution Limits

Contributions to other retirement savings vehicles, like 401(k)s and Individual Retirement Accounts, are strictly limited. Annuities, however, offer tremendous flexibility. One can contribute as much as he or she wants, to take advantage of triple compounding. Plus, an annuity contract can be added to at any time.

Flexible Payment Options

Unlike 401(k)s and IRAs, which require that withdrawals begin at age 70 ½ , one can wait much longer with annuities. When it is convenient to begin receiving payments, the following are methods that can be selected:

- Lump Sum distribution (a one-time payment)
- Periodic distributions (one can take money only when needed)
- Systematic distributions (a fixed amount is sent at regular intervals)

TAX CONTROL

The money inside an annuity is made up of two components—principal and earnings. Assuming the annuity was opened with after-tax dollars, only the earnings will be taxed. Different distribution methods behave differently when it comes to taxes; for instance, Lump Sum, Periodic, and Systematic distributions exhaust all earnings (which are taxable) before tapping principal. Under annuitization, each payment consists of both principal and interest, spreading tax liability evenly among payments. Through these distribution options, one has complete control over when taxes will be paid on earnings.

Annuities are not perfect when it comes to tax control. If an individual should pass away while an annuity is accumulating, all deferred taxes on growth will be due, reducing the annuity's value.

Accumulating Retirement Funds

RETIREMENT PLANNING is a key element in the financial planning process; to be effective, however, it should begin relatively early in life and involve a strategy of systematically accumulating retirement funds. Surely there is no financial goal more important than achieving a comfortable standard of living in retirement. In many respects, retirement planning captures the very essence of financial planning.

Forward looking, has an impact on both current and future standard of living, and if successful, can be highly rewarding and make a significant contribution to net worth.

Accumulating adequate retirement funds is a daunting task that takes careful planning. Like budgets, taxes, and investments, retirement planning is vital to one's financial plans. Yet it is difficult for most people under the age of 30 to develop a well-defined set of retirement plans. There are just too many years to go until retirement and too many uncertainties to deal with: inflation, social security, family size, the type of pension one receives and how much money one will have when he or she is ready to retire.

Working with Compound Interest

FIGURING RETIREMENT needs from the Inflation Multiplier Chart is taking advantage of tax-deferred growth in a retirement plan like an IRA, or a pension plan, 403 (b), or 401(k) plan at work. Taxes on the profits made from investments in these plans are deferred. The great part is not only deferring taxes, but also the fact that one makes profits on profits. This difference between investing taxable and tax deferred really adds up over time.

The earlier an individual starts growing their money for retirement, the better. If an individual places $2,000 a year in an IRA for just five years, for age 14 through age 18, and then never puts in another dime, that individual could retire at age 65 with a cool $1.184 million (assuming an average 10% return).

Retirement Portfolio in Accumulation Years (Ages 20–49)

Lizzie Ryan, a 28-year-old account manager for a communications firm, is just beginning to participate in her employer's 401(k) savings plan. Though relatively new to investing, Amanda realizes that she must accept some investment risk in order to reach her long-term retirement goals.

Initial Asset Allocation

Because Lizzie is in her early working years and, as a result, has a long time horizon, her asset allocation should be tilted toward stocks. Here's why:

- *Over time, stocks have provided better returns than the other primary asset classes (bonds and cash investments) and served as a better hedge against inflation.*
- *The longer one has to invest, the more time he or she has to weather the market's inevitable ups and downs. So, with a long time horizon, an individual is less likely to feel any permanent effects of market volatility—and more likely to see those better returns.*

With a 40-year time horizon, Lizzie could invest all of her 401(k) money in stocks. But Lizzie, like many people, does not have the stomach for such a commitment. A modest investment in bonds should help to reduce fluctuations in the value of Lizzie savings. The recommended allocation for Lizzie during her accumulation years: ***80% stocks/20% bonds.***

Retirement Portfolio for Transition Years (Ages 50–59)

Pete Randall, who just turned 56, works for an engineering consulting firm. Most of his retirement savings are invested in his firm's 401(k) plan, which offers various cash investment, bond, and stock options. Because of the decade-long bull market, Pete finds that stocks now make up more than 85% of his total retirement investments. Since he plans to retire at age 60, Pete wonders if his allocation is appropriate for this stage of his life.

An Initial Asset Allocation

PETE PLANS TO RETIRE in less than five years, so he needs to ensure that he will be able to maintain his standard of living throughout retirement.

While stocks should continue to make up a good portion of Pete's allocation, it's time to move some of his plan assets into more conservative options, such as cash investments and bonds. Pete could keep his allocation as is, but a major emphasis on stocks may not be good for investors who will be drawing on those investments within five years. A lengthy stock market decline could mean fewer assets for Pete when he needs them most, at retirement. The recommended allocation for Pete during his transition years: ***60% stocks/40% bonds.***

Chapter 2

Setting Sail for Your Estate Plan

The Financial Strategy for an Estate

BOTH OF THESE APPROACHES might work at times, but each can be quite costly. There is a better way.

Some advocate a process for making decisions about personal financial planning. There are some questions to be understood and then answered with relative ease by following this process. The process involves six steps:

- *identify the goals*
- *gather the data and make assumptions*
- *evaluate the feasibility of the goals*
- *develop strategies*
- *implement the decisions*

- *review the progress*

Identify the Goals

The starting point of a successful estate plan, as with any area of financial planning, is identifying and defining goals. What is the most appropriate way to dispose of one's assets at his or her death? Who will receive what, and when will they receive it? Will assistance in the management of the assets be required? If there are minor children, an individual must consider who will care for them and with what financial resources. How can the costs of administering an estate, including taxes, be minimized? Has an agent been appointed to act on one's behalf in the event of his or her disability? Will the family be adequately provided for in the event of the breadwinner's premature death?

Gather the Data and Make Assumptions

After identifying goals, one can begin to gather data. An individual will need to collect current estate planning documents, including wills and trust instruments, beneficiary designations on retirement plans and insurance policies, and title documents that set out the ownership of major assets such as a home. In addition, one will need to quantify the value of assets and liabilities. This individual must also consider non-financial issues, such as asset management and protection and the timing of when wants assets to ultimately pass to heirs.

Evaluate the Feasibility of Goals

Most goals dealing with the disposition of assets can be accomplished with estate planning. However, one cannot completely control how heirs spend their inheritance. Similarly, in larger estates, some amount of estate taxes may be incurred, even with planning. It may not be possible to meet goals of complete control or elimination of taxes.

Develop Strategies

Identify the planning documents that must be drafted or revised. Determine which tax planning strategies may be appropriate. Consider the individuals or entities to which the assets will be entrusted after one's death. Assess the needs of a family members—including spouse, parents, children, and grandchildren.

Implement the Decisions

Effective decision-making is more than a matter of saying "yes" or "no;" one's decision is meaningless until an individual turns his or her words into deeds. In this step, one implements the strategies that have been developed. Assign specific tasks to family members, and determine whether professional assistance from tax advisers, attorneys, trust officers, or insurance representatives is needed.

Review Progress

This final step is easy to ignore, but it is among the most critical. Few decisions are static; we base our choices on a series of events and circumstances that can and do change.

Every few years or after a major life event—a marriage, adoption or birth of a child, death of a child or spouse, disability, serious illness, inheritance, divorce, retirement, or career change—one should reconsider the various aspects of a plan. Have goals changed? Have new and better options become available? Are there better ways to do what must be done? Don't be afraid to revise goals, gather more data, reconsider choices, make new strategies, or carry out original strategies differently.

Estate planning is a lifelong process in that one evaluates a situation and plan for the future. It includes planning for retirement, for the possibility of disability, and for death. The estate planning process requires that an individual consider a wide range of legal, financial, emotional, and logistical issues.

Estate planning can be a positive experience, since it involves reviewing various situations and planning for the future. Although most people also find it unpleasant to think about the possibility of disability or death, advance planning is also a way to show love and to reduce potential distress later.

Most people don't realize that they are likely to spend at least 25% of their life in retirement. It's no easy trick going from full time productive work to retirement. The drama of the "golden years" is often shattered by the reality of not enough money to really enjoy retirement the way it was envisioned. Most people when it comes to retirement planning forget to take into account inflation. They are surprised at how much just a three or four percent inflation rate per year will affect costs by the time they retire.

The mere mention of certain words—such as "family," "death," or "disability"—can evoke a wide range of emotions from anyone. Such emotions can help motivate people to plan for the future, but can also interfere with proper estate planning.

When a family member or friend dies, there is a natural process of grieving, that can interfere with our ability to make decisions. In addition, grief can sometimes impact already-strained family relationships. A person's death often terminates or changes relationships, especially if the deceased person was the only common link between other people. For example, a surviving spouse may have less contact with the deceased spouse's children from a prior marriage.

Many of the emotions we feel after someone's death are natural, healthy, and probably unavoidable. However, some emotional problems could be reduced or eliminated by advance planning. And consideration of the impact of probate proceedings and estate taxes can often avoid hardships.

Death is not the only event one should plan for. Due to illness or accident, many people become incapacitated, either for brief periods or permanently, and cannot make their own decisions. If an individual is disabled, family and friends will be emotionally distraught and yet may need to make very important decisions.

Making decisions for an incapacitated person is always difficult. The person making the decisions will feel more comfortable if the incapacitated person has left advance instructions and has selected a specific person to make decisions. Estate planning must address the emotional needs of family, friends, and oneself.

Techniques For Estate Strategy

THERE ARE A NUMBER of “advanced” estate planning techniques that can reduce estate taxes, but every planning technique has unique benefits and drawbacks. For example, some estate-planning experts advocate the use of a limited partnership or other techniques. Special valuation rules sometimes allow a larger fractional interest to be transferred tax-free if a business or property is held through a separate legal entity. These entities can be ideal estate-planning tools for a "family business" or for large real estate holdings.

However, property that is given away before death does not receive an “adjusted basis,” so the gift and estate tax benefits of limited partnerships usually result in much larger capital-gains income tax bills if the partnership assets are later sold. (This is acceptable if the capital gains tax is less than the estate tax saved.) Some techniques may involve painful side effects (e.g., taxes on “phantom income”), and all create substantial accounting burdens.

The use of "business trusts" or even more unusual "offshore" trusts or other offshore legal entities is sometimes appropriate for a very limited group of individuals. The high cost and likelihood of legal challenges make this technique unsuitable for most people.

If an individual believes that advanced estate-planning techniques are appropriate for his or her situation, it is important to make sure to consult with attorneys who are familiar with both the estate planning and business aspects of such techniques.

Giving Today, Not Tomorrow

One of the easiest ways to provide for loved ones is by making annual gifts. Gifting today not only reduces an estate, but also allows one to share in the joy a gift can bring.

Each and every U.S. citizen can give away up to $10,000 per person each year. A husband and wife together can give $20,000 to any child, grandchild... or anyone else they feel like. For instance, if a couple has three children and 8 grandchildren, they can gift a total of $220,000 (11 beneficiaries x $20,000) per year, completely free of gift and inheritance taxes.

With the passage of the Taxpayer Relief Act of 1997, Congress began raising the $10,000 limit to account for inflation. However, as politicians often do, they put some restrictions on the increases. Congress stipulated that the $10,000 limit would rise with inflation, rounded down to the nearest thousand.

Suppose inflation is 3%; the limit would rise to $10,300 but be rounded down to $10,000. The next year, it would rise to $10,630, only to be rounded down again to $10,000.

Give Too Much?

What happens if an individual gifts too much (i.e., over the $10,000 "annual gift exclusion")? The beneficiary will have to pay taxes on the amount over $10,000. These taxes can rise as high as 55%, and closely mirror estate tax rates.

An alternative is to have the amount over $10,000 apply towards a Unified Credit. Everyone is given this credit by the IRS, and it is usually used for calculating estate taxes. Currently, the Unified Credit shelters $675,000 of the estate from taxes. If a daughter is given $50,000 (and only $10,000 is possible to gift), then the remaining $40,000 could be subtracted from the Unified Credit. The Unified Credit will be reduced to $635,000 but the daughter will not be taxed on the gift.

Another concern when gifting is that an individual gives away too much of the estate, not to trigger a tax, but to maintain a lifestyle. Many people automatically gift and end up giving too much of their assets to loved ones. Gifting should always be part of an overall estate plan that considers current needs. Before writing the annual gift check, it is important to check with an estate advisor.

Setting Up a Living Trust

At the very least, no matter how much one wants to give a family should consider setting up a Living Trust. Living Trusts allow one to avoid probate, maintain privacy, and facilitate the transferring of assets. Living Trusts also help married couples to maximize both of their Unified Credits. Living Trusts are simple to create, usually costing anywhere from $500-$1,500 (depending on the complexity of the estate). A practicing estate attorney can help draft one, or review one if it is already drawn up.

Consider Estate Taxes

Many people do not consider estate taxes when setting up an estate plan. Estate tax rates, like gift taxes, can climb as high as 55%. Effectively funding a trust with tax-advantaged vehicles, like municipal bonds and cash-rich life insurance, can help reduce taxes even more.

A Family's Goals and Objections

The best thing that an elderly individual can do to provide for his or her family is to talk with them about what he or she wants to accomplish. Is it important for all the grandchildren to go through college? How is the best way to have personal property divided? How should the money be used? The more one communicates with trusted family members, the greater chances the estate will be divided up evenly.

Chapter 3

Setting Sail with Living Trusts

THE INDIVIDUAL WHO is setting up the living trust is the grantor/settlor who establishes a written revocable trust agreement, naming himself or herself as the beneficiary while the individual is alive and family members or others as beneficiaries after his or her death. As such the grantor maintains full and absolute control over assets and he or she can revoke or change the trust at any time.

The trust is funded during the lifetime of the grantor by the transfer of all assets to it. Almost any kind of property one owns can be placed in the trust—bank accounts, stocks, bonds, and real estate. The grantor simply places the property in the trust by changing the name or title of the asset to the name of the trust. As such, no control is lost since the grantor designates himself or herself as the trustee and therefore continues to manage and handle the property as before.

Considering The Types of Beneficiaries

The Role of an IRA as a Beneficiary

THE LIVING TRUST HAS no life expectancy since it is not a person but a trust. Therefore, when an IRA owner dies, if all the benefits are paid into the living trust, as the beneficiary, the total amount of the plan immediately becomes subject to income tax. However, on December 30, 1997, the Department of the Treasury issued a proposed modification to Proposed Regulation Section 1.401 (2)(a)-1, D-5, which would allow a revocable living trust to be used in the same manner as irrevocable trusts to be the beneficiary of a retirement plan, if the requirements of the proposed regulations, as modified are met. The proposed regulations require than:

- The trust becomes irrevocable upon the IRA owner's death.
- A copy of the trust must be provided to the plan administrator.
- The IRA owner must agree to provide the plan administrator with any future trust amendments.
- A certified list of all trust beneficiaries must be provided to the plan administrator. The IRA owner must also agree to provide any corrected certification when changes occur and must agree to provide a copy of the trust instrument if requested by the plan administrator. If there is more than one beneficiary, the life expectancy of the oldest beneficiary is used to calculate the required minimum distributions.

The Role of the Designated Beneficiary

A designated beneficiary is a special IRS concept that is used to determine the length of time over which the benefits of a qualified plan must be paid after the death of a participant. A designated beneficiary is generally defined as an individual who is named as a beneficiary under the terms of a qualified plan or who is named as the beneficiary in a participant's beneficiary designation. Not every beneficiary who receives plan benefits meets the requirements of a designated beneficiary.

The period over which payments from the plan can be taken after the death of the participant can be longer in cases where there is a designated beneficiary. This period of time varies, depending on whether the participant began taking payments from the plan prior to his or her death. Without a designated beneficiary, the ability to take the proceeds into income over the life expectancy of a spouse or a beneficiary is lost, which means the benefit of deferring income tax may be lost.

If there is not a designated beneficiary and the participant received payments under the plan, only the participant's life expectancy can be used for determining the period over which his or her benefits must be paid. If there is not a designated beneficiary and the participant dies before taking payments from the plan, then the entire proceeds from the qualified plan must be paid out within five years of the date of the participant's death.

Considering Types of Living Trust

The Role of The "A" Living Trust

The "A" trust, a regular trust, can be used for single persons or married couples, but is more advisable, from the standpoint of better estate planning and estate tax savings, to be used when only one person is involved. Usually under the "A" trust, for estates valued less than $600,000, the entire estate will flow down to the heirs; because it is small, the entire estate also will incur no estate tax or probate fees; for estates valued more than $600,000, however, taxes will be due.

The Role of The "A-B" Living Trust

AN "A-B" LIVING TRUST is a particular form of living trust which is usable by any two individuals, married or unmarried, whereby when the first party dies, this trust automatically splits into two separate parts of the same trust, with one part, referred to as the "A" Trust, pertaining to the surviving party or spouse, and the other part, the "B" Trust, pertaining to the deceased party or spouse. Thus, with the couple's assets placed into an "A-B" trust, upon the death of one individual, one-half of the assets will flow down into a separate division of the same trust, the "B" (decedent's) trust. Thus, the trick here is that both spouses shall have preserved both federal estate tax equivalent exemptions ($600,000 each) and would have thus avoided liability for any estate taxes for that amount of estate value.

The Role of The "A-B-C" Living Trust

THE "A-B-C" TRUST CAN be used only by married couples, and not by a mate in a non-martial relationship. But briefly defined, the "A-B-C", also called the "Q-TIP" Trust, the IRS jargon for "Qualified Terminal Interest Property," is the final variant of the living trust whose specific purpose and advantage is one thing and one thing alone: namely, to enable the surviving spouse to postpone payment of any estate taxes that would have otherwise been due on the first spouse's property when the first spouse dies, until the death of the second spouse – regardless of the size of the estate.

The "C" part of the "A-B-C" trust device is simply a way to postpone paying estate taxes if one's estate is more than $1.2 million in value. A simpler understanding of the concept involved, assume that one has a combined estate worth in excess of $1.2 million in net value. This person probably already has the "A-B" trust, so he or she should have already taken advantage of the two estate tax exemptions of $600,000 each – or up to the $1.2 million maximum limit of exemptions allowed. Since this individual has an estate worth in excess of $1.2 million, what he or she needs to do is to create or add a "C" part of the trust so that one can place that excess over the $1.2 million in the "C" trust and at least be able to delay payment of the taxes due on that part of the estate.

Considering Asset Management

A LIFETIME ADVANTAGE of a living trust is that it allows one to retain professionals to manage its investments. Although a professional trustee is not required, the option is open. If the beneficiaries are young or financially naïve, the attraction of professional management is even greater because, after one's death, the trustee will be there to protect the assets until the beneficiaries are able to exercise responsible judgment on their own. Designating a professional trustee also gives one the opportunity to see how they will manage the living trust. If the grantor does not like how, it is being managed, changes can be made.

A Living Trust provides management of assets if one becomes physically or mentally incapacitated. While able-minded, an individual is designated in the Trust Agreement as a successor trustee who assumes responsibility for managing assets should that individual become incapacitated. At the time of incapacity only simple documentation in required for the successor trustee to assume his/her responsibilities and no "conservatorship" resulting from court intervention is needed.

Considering Strategies for Transferring Assets

OWNERSHIP OF ASSETS must be transferred from one's name to the Living Trust. Listing assets and insurance in a Schedule A for a Trust is absolutely meaningless in terms of funding the Trust. The Grantor needs to transfer the title of all his assets into the Living Trust. Otherwise, a Trust is not funded.

If the assets are not recorded in the name of the Trust, the Trust effectively becomes nothing more than a will. On the death of a spouse, the assets must still go through probate before they can pass into the Trust. Items that should be transferred into the Trust include real estate, stocks, bonds, and savings accounts.

The Role of Checking Accounts

CHECKING ACCOUNTS SHOULD be transferred to the Trust. An individual should go to an officer of the bank and insist they record his checking account in the name of his Living Trust, but also insist that the checks still read the same as before. This way, the checking account is in the Living Trust and avoids the possibility of probate.

When the Grantor transfers his checking account into the Trust the name of the Trust does not need to be printed on the face of the checks. If the Trust name is printed on the checks he may encounter difficulties writing checks because he will have to sign as "Trustee" and people unfamiliar with Living Trusts may refuse to honor the check.

The Role of Transferring Deeds

PROPER TRANSFER IS critical to avoid future problems. The transfer will not accelerate one's mortgage, nor will it cause his mortgage to become due once the deed is properly transferred. Also, it will not cause a change in his property taxes, and the state tax exemption or the state. Homestead exemption is not affected by placing his home into the Trust. Additionally, the $250,000 exemption is not affected by putting the home into the Trust.

The Role of Transferring a Business Interest

THE TYPE OF BUSINESS (corporation, partnership or proprietorship) determines how this transfer is best achieved. With corporation stock, the company's transfer agent should change the ownership of his stock from his name to the name of the Trust. A privately owned corporation is easily transferred by voiding their existing stock certificates and reissuing new stock certificates in the name of the Trust.

To transfer a newly formed limited partnership interest, the ownership on the units should be in the name of the Trust. If the limited partnership interests have already been issued, the general partner should grant the limited partner permission to transfer the interest into the Trust. On rare occasions, a general partner may decline to transfer one's limited partnership interest into the Trust. Legal counsel can resolve this by creating a Bill of Sale/Letter of Transfer for one's interest, if the General Partner is really reluctant to make a transfer.

Transferring a business interest into the Trust does not restrict the owners in their ownership capacities. There are great advantages to owning the business in the Trust, because the surviving trustee or successor trustee would simply take over in case of incapacity, and would be authorized to sell quickly after the death of a principal. On the death of an owner, a partnership or sole proprietorship perishes. The only recourse for the survivors is to sell quickly, which may be impossible during the probate process. The quick and easy solution is to place the business in a Living Trust.

The Role of Transferring Qualified Retirement Plans

Qualified retirement plans generally include company pension and profit sharing plans, employee stock ownership plans (ESOPs), individual retirement plans (IRAs), and simplified employee pension plans (SEPs). A revocable living trust can be named as the beneficiary of a qualified retirement plan as long as provisions of the Internal Revenue Code and its regulations are met. A trustee of a living trust may elect the form of the benefit to be received by the plan. By naming the trust as the beneficiary of a plan, the tax benefits that are chosen will inure to the benefit of the beneficiaries of the trust. The benefits selected are not impaired by naming a revocable living trust as a beneficiary.

Since the beneficiary of qualified plan proceeds must pay income tax on them as income with respect to a decedent—income that was due the decedent but which was not paid during his or her life—naming a living trust as beneficiary can also allocate this income in such a manner as to reduce federal estate tax upon the death of the surviving spouse. This is an important planning consideration in many estates.

While it is true that qualified plan proceeds paid directly to a beneficiary, including a living trust, avoid probate on the death of the plan participant, it is not uncommon for the beneficiary designation to name the participant's probate estate as the beneficiary. While this procedure is legal, it is bad planning because the proceeds will be subject to probate and may also be subject to the claims of creditors. This incident would not happen if a living trust were the recipient of the proceeds.

The Role of Assets Not Readily Transferred to a Living Trust

There are four types of assets that for different reasons may present difficulties if they are held in the name of a living trust. Trust critics sometimes cite the problems of funding a living trust with these assets as proof that living trust do not work well. Each of these assets is unique and can present funding difficulties. These difficulties can often be overcome with proper living trust—centered planning. They are listed here:

- ***Homestead Property***
    - Homestead exemptions are personal in nature and a subject to statutory restrictions as to their use. As a result, there is a question as to whether or not a residence that transferred into a living trust will continue to qualify under a state's homestead law. Most states have no law on whether a homestead exemption is preserved or lost if the homestead is transferred to a living trust.

- ***Professional Corporation Stock***
    - Stockholders of professional corporations are required by state law to be licensed members of their profession.

The purpose of the laws restricting the transfer of professional corporation stock to people who are not members of the profession is to assure the public that laypersons are not involved in making decisions that should be made only by licensed professionals. It depends on state law whether professional corporation stock may be held in a revocable trust either while the professional is living or during the winding up of his or her affairs after death.

- ***Section 1244 Stock***
    - Section 1244 of the Internal Revenue Code provides that a loss on the sale of exchange of the common stock of a small business corporation which would otherwise be treated as a capital loss, will be treated as an ordinary loss if certain conditions are met. Even though the favorable capital gains income tax rate was eliminated by the Tax Reform Act of 1986, the restrictions on taking capital losses were retained. An ordinary loss can be offset against all income in a year and may be either carried forward or carried back.

- Section 1244 stock is routinely issued to business owners who incorporate their new or existing business ventures. The ordinary loss treatment of stock under Section 1244 is allowed only to individuals and to partnerships which have continuously held the stock from the date of its issuance. Because a transfer of stock to a living trust will disqualify if for Section 1244 treatment, the determination as to the importance of Section 1244 as compared to the benefits provided by placing ownership of the stock in a living trust is a question than must be resolved.

- ***Section 1244 Stock and S Corporations***
    - Section 1244 is of less importance to many corporate stockholders than it was in the past. Beginning in the late 1970s and culminating in the Tax Reform Act of 1986, congress eliminated most of the reasons to use a regular corporation for the small business owner. Many companies that were incorporated as regular corporations have been converted to S Corporations.

- The original purpose of Section 1244 was to put a regular corporation's stockholders on par with sole proprietors or members of a partnership. A sole proprietor or a partner can deduct the operating losses sustained in a business. These ordinary losses offset their other income. A stockholder of a regular corporation cannot deduct corporate losses; they are only deductible against the corporation's income.

- ***Stock Option***
    - Stock options that are held in a revocable living trust will avoid probate on the owner's death and financial guardianship if the owner becomes disabled. Because of the uncertainties in the tax law about stock options, it is important to balance the need for living trust-centered planning with the potential pitfalls of will-planning to the uncertainty of the tax laws.

The Internal Revenue Code provides special income tax advantages for certain qualified stock options and purchase plans. Under the Code, a person who receives stock from a qualified stock option plan does not have to take the value of stock received into income when he or she receives it. These plans require certain holding periods.

Considering the Living Trust Provisions

The Role of the Marital Deduction Provision

The marital deduction is a provision under the tax laws that allows a reduction in estate taxes when one dies, if this individual is married. Based on the concept that a married couple is one economic unit, and that the estate tax should therefore be postponed until the death of the second spouse, the marital deduction works this way. Upon the death of the first spouse, one can leave any amount of assets, even to 100% to the spouse and it will not be taxed at the death of the first spouse, thus allowing the family the use of the funds during the life of the surviving spouse.

Transfers of terminable interests or interests that terminate upon the happening of a certain event, such as the remarriage of a surviving spouse, or the passage of time, do not qualify for a marital deduction. Exceptions to these include qualified terminable interest property (QTIP), power-of-appointment trusts, and if the period of time that a spouse must survive the deceased spouse does not exceed six months.

Property passing to the surviving spouse as a joint tenant by right of survivorship, through dower or curtest interests, under powers of appointment, and by transfers made during one's lifetime that are included in the gross estate, all qualify for the marital deduction. The deduction also applies to life insurance proceeds paid outright to the surviving spouse or to a trust which itself qualifies for the marital deduction.

The Role of the Unified Credit Provision

A unified credit is allowed against the estate tax. The tax credit exempts the transfer of property from estate tax. The amount of the credit that is not used will be lost. For a married couple, the way the exemption is utilized can have a positive result of estate tax savings. This tax can be avoided by creating a trust in the amount of the exemption for the benefit of the surviving spouse, who would receive all income there from and the principal, if necessary.

Upon the death of the second spouse, the property in the trust will pass to the next generations, estate tax free. The benefits from the trust can also be sprinkled or sprayed among children and grandchildren in addition to the surviving spouse. If both spouses create such a plan, then upon the death of the survivor of them, they can effectively pass property having a value equal to both exemptions to their heirs, estate tax free.

The Role of the Benefit Provision

The benefits of having a living trust are many. A Living Trust avoids time and expense of probate when the individual dies. It avoids multiple probates if there is real estate in more than one state. It allows an easier, more efficient management of the estate. It prevents court control of assets if one becomes physically or mentally incapacitated. It gives maximum privacy. It can reduce or eliminate estate taxes. It allows quicker distribution of assets to beneficiaries.

It prevents the court from controlling assets when minor children inherit. It prevents unintentional disinheriting. It is more difficult than a will to contest. It provides an effective prenuptial protection. It is easy to set up. It can be canceled or changed at any time. It gives maximum control while living, and after death also.

Considering Methods of Funding a Living Trust

Only assets titled in the name of a living trust avoid probate or guardianship proceedings. The process of re-titling assets in the name of the trust is called funding. A Living trust that contains all of its maker's property is called a fully funded living trust. A living trust which contains little of its maker's property is called an unfounded living trust.

The purpose of an unfounded trust, sometimes called a "standby trust," is to be available for funding in the event the maker becomes incapacitated or determines that the trust should only be funded as a last-minute pre-death precaution. Un-funded living trusts are almost always named as the beneficiary of the maker's life insurance policies. Property that is not put into an unfounded living trust during the lifetime of a maker is put there after death by the maker's pour-over will. The funding and maintenance costs of unfounded trusts are by definition nonexistent or minimal.

The Role of General Funding Principles

Usually, the same form of document by which the property was received by the trust maker should be used to transfer the property to the living trust. Deeds are used to transfer real property into living trusts. Bills of sale are used for transferring personal effects. Assignments are commonly used to transfer intangible personal property, such as partnership interests and non-publicly traded stocks into living trusts. Publicly traded stocks and bonds are endorsed to trusts, and new certificates are generated in the name of the trust. For vehicles, boats, brands for livestock, and other property interests that have special types of ownership, the title is changed by complying with local statutes.

Because a revocable living trust is not a separate income tax entity, and because it is the alter ego of its maker, most state and local governments exempt the transfer of the maker's property into his or her trust from sales and use taxes. The same is true of documentary stamps required for the transfer of real estate.

The transfer of encumbered property to a living trust may present some initial practical problems. However, these problems are usually unfounded and arise from a creditor's lack of understanding of the transaction and living trusts in general. The law is clear that the debt on secured property follows the property, no matter to whom or where the property is transferred. A secured creditor cannot lose rights in the property when it is titled in the name of a living trust. The rules for conveying property to revocable living trusts vary from jurisdiction to jurisdiction. These jurisdictional variations apply because of differences in statutes and local customs. Living trusts are amazingly resilient and flexible documents that are designed to expedite the transfer of property, not to hinder it.

The Role of Funding With a Payable-On-Death Assignment

After-Death Assignment is another method for funding a living trust. This is a method to transfer some types of property into a living trust found in the Uniform Probate Code. The UPC provides that certain financial accounts such as bank saving accounts can be assigned at death without passing though probate. This form of assignment is called a Payable-On-Death assignment or "POD" designation. A POD designator can be used to fund a living trust on the death of its maker without probate and administration.

The drawback to assigning property under a POD is that if the maker becomes disabled, the property is held outside the trust. Thus, it is always wise to create a limited durable power of attorney that specifically allows the agent to transfer POD property to the trust.

The Role of Combining Funding Methods

Many professionals and clients believe that a single funding method must be selected and then utilized. This is a rigid viewpoint that is not accurate. Living trusts can be funded in a number of ways. Mixing funding options is totally acceptable and is often a practical necessity. Fully funding a living trust forces title issues into the open, where they can be dealt with before it is too late to take action to correct problems that might be unsolvable and unduly expensive after disability of death. During the funding process, a person not only finds out precisely what he or she owns but, more importantly, how he or she actually owns it. At that time, each asset can be reviewed in light of a person's estate and financial planning goals.

Living Trusts and Taxes

A Living Trust has no effect on local taxes. It will not change the valuation of one's home nor alter the homestead exemption in any way. Neither is there any effect on income taxes. In fact, while both spouses are alive, no tax return is filed for the Living Trust. Income taxes are reported on IRS 1040 form just as they have been reported for years.

If the trust maker is the sole trustee or a co-trustee of the trust, all of the income, deductions, and credits generated by the trust property are reported on the maker's personal income tax return. The maker's social security number is used as the federal taxpayer identification number of the trust. If the trust maker is not a trustee, a separate taxpayer identification number must be obtained for the trust, but the maker still reports all income, deductions, and credits or his or her personal income tax return. In this case, the trust is required to file an information return. A revocable living trust does not become a separate taxable entity until the death of its maker.

The Role of Income Taxes

INCOME TAXES ARE TAXES that are assessed or payable on one's income. They are taxes paid on income one might have earned or received during any period in one's lifetime, before death. For example, even after one dies, his or her estate may still be required to file a final federal income tax return and pay taxes due on it, if any, for any earnings one might had had, if any, for that portion of the final year in which one lived.

And, depending on the state or residence, one may also have to pay state income tax as well. On this type of tax, namely, the income tax, one needs to understand that the living trust will have no effect whatsoever for an individual. It will neither lower nor eliminate this type of tax.

The Role of Estate & Inheritance Taxes

THE OTHER TYPE OF TAX that everyone is concerned with is the federal estate tax and the state inheritance tax. In short, it is death taxes. With respect to the federal government, this is the type of tax the federal government (the IRS) levies on one's estate when he or she dies if the net value of the estate is more than $600,000 payable by the estate before it is distributed to one's beneficiaries. The "inheritance" tax is a state-imposed tax levied on the "right" to inherit, paid by the estate before any assets are distributed to the heirs.

There is a great deal of confusion concerning estate taxes. Estate taxes have nothing to do with the cost of probate or the cost of capital gains taxes. Estate taxes are assessed on the value of the assets transferred to heirs at the time of death. Estate taxes are there regardless of the technique in which one titles assets (sole ownership, joint ownership, corporation or trust). For almost two decades each person was allowed a $600,000 exemption on the total inheritances the person passed to his or her heirs. A heavy tax of 37% kicked in on any excess over $600,000 and graduated up to 55% when the excess hit $3-million.

In other words, a husband and wife each had a $600,000 exemption and, by using those exemptions wisely, could pass a total of up to $1.2 million to their children without any estate taxes. The exemption was increased to $625,000 per person on January 1, 1998, increased again to $650,000 on January 1, 1999 and went to $675,000 on January 1, 2000. The exemption continued to rise almost every year until it reached $1-million per person ($2-million for a married couple) in the year 2006.

Congress passed this new tax bill under "budget rules" which required an expiration or "sunset" date of 2010 when the temporary law would be repealed unless congress acted to make the cuts permanent. Late in 2010, congress passed another extension for two years for the tax cuts.

The "estate tax" is a special tax on property left by a deceased person. In the U.S., there are separate federal and state estate taxes, but most state death taxes, including California's, can be claimed as a credit against the federal estate tax. The overall estate tax rate thus remains uniform in most states. However, some states, including a few "retirement states," retain inheritance or estate taxes that are owed on smaller estates that are not subject to federal estate tax.

The Role of Federal Estate Tax

The Federal Estate Tax is a tax on any transfer of assets from a deceased person's estate to his or her heirs. President Bush signed a bill that slowly phased out the federal estate tax as of January 1, 2010. Although the tax bill provides for repeal of the estate tax, it also includes a "sunset provision," meaning that the entire tax bill was no longer valid at all after January 1, 2011.

However, there are some problems with this legislation:

- ***The estate tax was in effect until 2010.***

For budget reasons, the Congress has decided to slowly phase out the tax. This makes planning an estate difficult because many clients may assume that they don't need to plan to avoid the estate tax because they will live until 2010. That assumption will be correct for many, but those who are wrong are taking a gamble that might cost their estates several hundred thousand dollars.

- ***The estate tax after 2010***

Under the Economic Growth and Tax Relief Reconciliation Act of 2001, the federal estate tax was eliminated in 2010. The gift tax, however, remained in effect at a 35 percent rate. On Jan. 1, 2011, the estate tax returns. According to a new law enacted in December 2010, estates valued at $5 million or less are exempt from the tax. Estates worth more than $5 million are taxed at a 35% rate.

With the return of the estate tax in 2011, the stepped-up basis on inherited property also returned. This means that an asset's basis is its fair market value on the day of the original owner's death.

For individuals who died in 2010, the estate has the option of following the 2010 estate tax rules, meaning no tax due on the estate, but the carryover basis rule is in effect, or using the 2011 estate tax rules, which include a 35% tax on estates worth more than $5 million and stepped-up basis on bequeathed assets.

Considering Tax Saving Techniques Using Living Trusts

The Role of The Tax-Saving "A-B" Living Trust

Up until now we have been discussing what is known as a "common" Living Trust. When used by a married couple, each spouse is a co-grantor (maker) of a common trust. When one spouse dies, the survivor becomes the sole grantor of the trust in much the same way that joint ownership turns into sole ownership when one spouse dies. The survivor gains full control and has the right to change or amend any part of the (common) trust in any way he/she chooses but loses one of the two $675,000 estate tax exemptions.

The survivor's trust is known as Trust A while the decedent's trust is known as Trust B. The $2,000,000 exemption of the first spouse to die is used to shelter Trust B. The survivor's $675,000 exemption is put on hold and reserved to shelter Trust A when the survivor also dies a few years later. The couple can now take full advantage of both of their exemptions and by current 2001 standards pass up to $1.35 million to their heirs completely free of Federal Estate Taxes; $675,000 from one spouse and $675,000 from the other.

This ability of an A-B Living Trust to double the amount of available estate tax exemption should all by itself be reason enough to abandon joint ownership of assets immediately and get into a Living Trust. However, there are other major advantages to an A-B Trust - and. a few minor disadvantages:

The surviving spouse can spend both principal and income from his/her own Trust A in any manner; no restriction.

- Only the assets in Trust A can be attached should the surviving spouse be confined to a nursing home. When properly written, no nursing home or hospital can touch the funds in Trust B.
- The surviving spouse is permitted to spend all income earned by Trust B plus the greater of $5,000 or 5% of principal in Trust B every year in any manner, no matter how foolishly.
- Trust B becomes irrevocable at the death of the first spouse to die and cannot be changed at the whim of the surviving spouse as can happen with either a will or a common trust. Thus, the rights of the deceased spouse are protected even in death.
- The A-B Trust is also ideal for couples on their second marriages since each spouse, using a special memorandum, can place assets in the trust for the mutual enjoyment and use of both, but upon death must come out of the trust and be distributed to the heirs of the first marriage.

An A-B Trust can save large amounts in death taxes for families by allowing a husband and wife to shelter $1.2 million dollars from the tax man. This type of trust generally holds all of the couple's wealth and, at the time that one of them dies, splits into two trusts. These two trusts are often designated the "A" and the "B" trusts. The former holds the survivor's share of the assets and the latter the decedent's share. The survivor can do anything he or she desires with the "A" side and is the complete owner of it. The "B" side provides all of the income to the survivor and, if required for his support, the survivor can withdraw principal from it. But, under IRS rules, the "B" side must be irrevocable after the first spouse dies.

Some "Unified" Relief

Congress has created what it called "Unified Credit". The Unified Credit allows every American citizen to pass a certain amount of their estate to heirs tax-free. This credit can be used during one's lifetime, but is usually used after someone has died and the estate is being distributed. With the Taxpayer Relief Act of 1997 and the Tax Relief Act of 2001, the Unified Credit has gradually been increasing. In addition, the top estate tax rate will be decreasing until 2010, when estate and gift taxes are fully repealed.

Skipping a Generation Can Be Costly

When an individual gifts over $1 million to grandchildren, the IRS slaps a double tax on this individual. Also, the IRS treats such a gift as "two gifts in one" and slaps a 55% tax on the gift twice. When such a gift is hit once with a 55% tax. and then again with another 55% tax, the gift is effectively reduced by 80%. That means $1 million of hard-earned wealth immediately shrinks to $200,000 for heirs, with the remainder going to Uncle Sam. The word "taxes" strikes fear into hearts. In no uncertain terms, taxes are the means by which Uncle Sam confiscates the money for his or her own use. And taxes come in many different forms. Income, sales, excise, gift, estate, luxury, property, the list of different taxes goes on and on.

The Estate Tax System

SINCE 1987, FEDERAL estate taxes have been imposed on the estate of any person who dies leaving assets worth more than $600,000 excluding bequests to a surviving spouse or charity. In some cases, a married couple can leave $1.2 million to their heirs tax-free, but only if a special "exemption" or "bypass" trust is created pursuant to a will or living trust at the time of the first spouse's death. Only about 8% of estates owe any estate taxes; estate taxes generate about 1% of federal tax revenue. In 1994, the Republican "Contract With America" pledged to increase the amount of the "unified credit" to $750,000 over a three-year period, and to increase it annually thereafter based on the inflation rate. That promise was one of the first to be abandoned—probably because "dead people don't vote."

Bills have been introduced in Congress every year, seeking to increase the "unified credit" for estate and gift taxes, but the bills have historically died in committees because no one could suggest ways to offset the lost tax revenue. More than 50 bills to alter estate and gift taxes have been introduced in the current 105th Congress.

Cost-of-Living Increases for Annual Gift Tax Exclusion Amount and GSTs

The first $10,000 of gifts is excluded from gift taxes under current law; starting in 1999, that amount will be increased based on the cost of living. However, the increases will only be made in $1,000 increments, so that no increase is likely until the year 2001. The $1 million exemption from generation-skipping transfer (GST) taxes was increased in 1999, rounded to the nearest $10,000 increment (other provisions exempt some additional transfers from GST taxes).

Family-Owned Business Exclusion

Owners of "qualified family-owned businesses" will receive an additional exemption so that their estates may exclude up to $1.3 million from estate taxes. In contrast to the long deferral of the increase in regular estate tax exemption, this $1.3 million exemption for these generous, mostly-Republican, campaign contributors is effective for all decedents dying after December 31, 1997. To qualify, the decedent or members of her family must have owned and materially participated in the business for at least 5 of the 8 years immediately preceding death; the exemption may be "recaptured" if the heirs sell the business within 10 years after the date of death. Many other technical requirements also apply.

Considering The Types of Taxes

The Role of the Gift Tax

IF THE TRUST IS REVOCABLE, there are no gift taxes upon its creation, because the grantor maintains dominion and control over the trust. However, a taxable gift can inadvertently be made if the grantor becomes legally incapacitated during the term of the trust. In such event, the living trust then becomes irrevocable. The trust agreement can guard against this happening, by providing that any power of revocation will continue to be exercisable by the holder of the power of attorney after one becomes disabled. Or the other option is to retain a special power of appointment which is set forth in the living trust. Further, it can provide the right to dispose of providing for assets by a will.

Gift Tax Returns Binding on IRS

Section 506 of TRA '97 contains a provision that will give relief to many tax advisors: it provides that the IRS may not attempt to revalue gifts made in years before death, if gift tax returns were filed and the statute of limitations has expired on those returns. This solves the problem of having the IRS assert, at the time an estate tax return is filed, that the decedent's unified credit was eroded or gift taxes are owed for gifts made many decades earlier. It will impose an extra burden on the IRS to review and audit gift-tax returns for which no tax is due, if there is any possibility that the value of the gifted property has been understated for example, when valuing limited family partnership interests which are subject to "valuation adjustments" or "discounts" for various reasons. While the law will probably increase the audit rate for gift tax returns, it will provide more certainty to taxpayers and their advisors.

The Gift Tax and an Annual Exclusion

ALL GIFTS IN A CALENDAR year not sheltered by the annual exclusion, the marital deduction or the charitable deduction are subject to the gift tax. Because the estate and gift tax system is unified, the unified credit can be used for lifetime gifts, if not already used up. The tax rate schedule is the same as for the estate tax. There is a $10,000annual exclusion from the gift tax per donor and per donee. Thus a married couple can give a married child $40,000 per year by each parent giving their child $10,000 and each giving their son or daughter in law $10,000. This can be extremely powerful if the gifts are made to someone who will invest them for the long term. Unlimited transfers for educational and medical expenses are also excluded from gift tax so long as they are made directly to the provider.

Capital-Gains Exemption of $500,000 from Sale of Residence

The new law contains provisions that will exempt the first $250,000 (single) or $500,000 (married couple) of profits from the sale of property used as the principal residence for 2 of 5 years from capital gains taxes. While this provision does not directly affect the estate or gift tax laws, it will alter the computation of benefits from certain estate planning techniques, and it may dramatically change behaviors and thus impact estate planning. Many taxpayers have remained in homes much larger than they need because they wanted to avoid capital gains taxes that would be incurred if they "moved down" to a smaller and less expensive home. The new law is much more expansive than the former one-time $125,000 exclusion for persons over 55.

The Role of the Generation Skipping Tax

A TAX IS IMPOSED ON every gratuitous generation-skipping transfers ("GSTT"),whether made during life, at death or at the termination or distribution of a trust. The GSTT is in addition to the estate and gift tax on the transfer. The term "skip person" is often used to describe transferees whose receipt of a gift causes imposition of the tax. For gifts within families, skip persons are relatives two generations or more younger than the transferor (with the same rule applying to relatives of the transferor's spouse).

Non-relatives may also be skip persons with generation assignment being on the basis of date of birth. If born within 12.5 years of the transferor, the transferee is of the same generation. More than 12.5 years means the next generation. Then every twenty-five years is a new generation. Trusts may also be skip persons if all the present interests are skip persons. A predeceased parent exception allows for an adjustment where the transferee is the child of a deceased descendant of the transferor.

Every individual is entitled to a lifetime exemption for generation-skipping transfers of $1,000,000, which was indexed for inflation after 1998. Most planning in this area revolves around avoiding the tax and maximizing the use of the two exemptions available to a married couple. If all the transfers to a trust are protected by exemption allocations, no distributions from that trust will ever be subject to the tax, no matter how many generations are involved or how much the trust grows.

If some of the transfers are not protected by exemption allocations, a proportionate share of each distribution will be subject to the tax. So, the executor might be instructed to create two separate trusts, one of which will be allocated the remaining exemption. Different investment strategies can be considered for the two trusts to manage, to some extent, the effect of this onerous tax.

The Role of Excess Distribution & Excess Retirement Accumulation Tax

Section 1073 of TRA '97 repeals Internal Revenue Code section 4980A, which imposed a 15% penalty on portions of certain large withdrawals and on the balance of "over-funded" retirement accounts at death. At one time action by Congress partially suspended the "excess distribution" provisions of section 4980A for lifetime distributions, for three years only, in an effort to induce some taxpayers to accelerate distributions and thus ordinary income tax payments. By also repealing the excess accumulation provisions, Congress has eliminated an incentive to accelerate lifetime distributions.

The Role of the Estate Tax

THE GROSS ESTATE INCLUDES all assets in which a grantor has an interest, whether beneficial or otherwise. Upon one's death, the fair market value of the assets in the living trust will be included in the estate for estate tax purposes. If an individual has made a gift of trust property within three years of the date of the grantor's death, the question of whether these assets are included in the gross estate depends upon the terms of the trust. Gifts made by the grantor from his or her living trust in which the grantor was the sole beneficiary are not included. If the grantor is the sole beneficiary of the living trust, however, gifts made by the trust within three years of one's death could be included in the estate for estate tax purposes.

The Role of Federal Estate Taxes

The federal estate tax is an excise tax imposed on the right to transfer property at death. They are the taxes on any transfer of assets from a deceased person's estate to his or her heirs. As such, it taxes literally everything that a person owns including joint tenancy property, life insurance death proceeds, ownership in a business, and almost anything else that one can think of. All of the assets owned by the deceased person are subject to the tax, including property in joint tenancy, living trusts, and life insurance. Each estate has an exclusion from the tax that increased each year until 2006, when it became $1,000,000.

Only a handful of property interests are not subject to the federal estate tax, but they are rare. Property that avoids probate does not necessarily avoid the federal estate tax. Probate has nothing to do with the federal estate tax.

Considering Tax Planning Techniques

Most people go through life on financial autopilot, surfing blindly atop a wave of debts and expenses, hoping – sometimes vainly – that their income will keep them afloat. This does not just happen to people with modest incomes. Think of all the sports heroes, rock stars – even royalty – who've made millions, spent even more, then had to give up early retirement and rejoin us working stiffs.

That's the attractiveness of financial planning. If an individual knows how much money he or she has – and ideas how to use it – it's easy to make smart financial decisions. This informed individual will stop frittering away a promising financial future, and put money to work instead. If one socked away between 5% and 10% of take-home pay, either investing it intelligently or simply paying off old debts, individuals might just find that their dreams are within reach.

The Role of "Pour-Ups" for After-Death Income Tax Planning

WHILE IT IS CLEAR THAT a probate estate has relatively few substantive after-death income tax advantages over a trust, it may be advisable or necessary to create a probate estate for purposes of after-death income tax planning. This can be accomplished by pouring-up certain assets from a living trust to a probate estate. This technique is sometimes called reverse funding. It allows the probate estate to have the appropriate assets and income so that after-death income tax benefits can be used.

Pour-ups are discretionary distributions from a maker's revocable living trust to the maker's probate estate. The trust is used "as a vehicle for funneling funds to the executor when the executor is in need. In reality, a pour-up distribution is one where the trustee is authorized or directed to pay to the executor such sums as the executor requires for debts, expenses of administration, taxes and legacies. There should be significant after-death income tax advantages to justify the expense of creating a probate estate. The pour-up technique may have disadvantages other than this expense.

The Role of Federal Estate Tax Planning

UNDER CURRENT LAW THE estate tax exemption is scheduled to drop significantly from $5,000,000 to $1,000,000 and the estate tax rate is scheduled to jump from 35% to 55%, both effective January 1, 2013. While the federal estate tax exemption has been set at $5,000,000 and the estate tax rate was set at 35% for the 2010, 2011 and 2012 tax years, on January 1, 2013 the exemption and rate are scheduled to revert back to the numbers that were in effect in 2002 - which, as mentioned above, means a $1,000,000 exemption and 55% estate tax rate.

Some living trust advocates make the claim that a revocable living trust is superior to a will in terms of accomplishing federal estate tax planning. Will-planning and probate advocates take exception to this claim. They emphatically deny that the living trust can accomplish more effective estate planning than will planning.

The provisions of a properly drafted will can create exactly the same federal estate tax planning benefits that a living trust can. A testamentary trust and a revocable living trust can accomplish identical estate planning results. But testamentary planning often does not constitute good federal estate tax planning. It can only achieve maximum federal estate tax planning for married couples if it controls the property of the first spouse to die. And while wills have the capability to carry out federal estate tax planning, in reality they do not actually fulfill that capability.

Funded Living Trusts and Federal Estate Tax

Funded living trusts assure that many federal estate tax problems will be prevented. A living trust's federal estate tax formula clause will control more property than the typical formula clause will control more property than the typical formula clause in a will. This characteristic is especially important if the client and the attorney have not spent the time and energy to examine and re-title assets correctly.

Federal Estate Tax and The Unlimited Marital Deduction

For married couples, the Internal Revenue Code offers a method to defer federal estate tax called the Unlimited Marital Deduction. The unlimited marital deduction shelters all property left to a surviving spouse from federal estate tax when his or her spouse dies.

FORMULA CLAUSES FOR Federal Estate Tax Planning

There are two types of formula clauses that are typically used in federal estate tax planning for married couples. The two are as follows:

- Pecuniary Clause
- Fractional Share of the Residue Clause

Sometimes, when qualified plan proceeds are allocated to a marital trust or a family trust by a pecuniary bequest in a will or a trust, the allocation accelerates all of the income tax due on the proceeds. This acceleration can occur because of the special rules relating to the transfer of income in respect of a decedent.

Glossary

ADEQUATE PROTECTION—The standard of protection granted a creditor by the trustee or debtor-in-possession in order to avoid court sanctioned foreclosure on its property.

Administrator—The person appointed by the court to manage an estate when he or she dies without leaving a will. Since they are court appointed, they are required to post a bond as security. They have the same duties as an executor.

Amendment—This refers to a revision or addition to a trust document which either corrects an error, or changes the terms of the trust to coincide with the trustor's wishes.

Annual Exclusion—An exclusion from gift taxes for gifts by each donor to each donee, which is available on an annual basis. The annual exclusion is currently $10,000 per donee (and is indexed for inflation), per calendar year. That is, a couple with three children could give $60,000 per year tax free to the next generation. In order to qualify for the annual exclusion, the gift must be a "present interest" i.e., a gift available immediately to the donee as opposed to one not available until the future or one requiring the consent of some other person.

Applicable Credit Amount—An estate tax credit based upon the applicable exemption amount used to reduce the tax on transfers of property either during life (gift tax) or at death (estate tax). Created by the Taxpayer Relief Act of 1997, the applicable credit amount is $1,730,800 for 2011 and 2012.

Applicable Exemption Amount—For deaths occurring in 2011, up to $5,000,000 can be passed from an individual (for married couples, the applicable amount is $10,000,000) upon his or her death without incurring estate tax.

Attorney-in-fact—This refers to the individual who is designated in the power of attorney document to act on behalf of another.

Automatic Stay—An injunction, or court order, that takes effect when a bankruptcy petition is filed. An automatic stay prohibits all collection against a debtor.

Asset—The property of a testator or grantor, whether real or personal, which passes under a will and/or is placed into a trust account.

Asset Allocation—Investment assets can be placed into different categories for classification purposes. When an Investment Advisor assigns a percentage of the account investments to each of these categories, he is completing an Asset Allocation. Asset Allocation is an acceptable way for a manager or trustee to diversify risk and increase return in an investment portfolio.

Assignment—This is a document that assigns the interest of one party to another. When a grantor wants to place a contract or lease into a trust, an assignment of the grantor's interest is prepared to transfer the interest to the trust. The Assignor is the one conveying the interest and the Assignee is the one receiving the interest.

Avoidance Powers—The powers used by a trustee to reverse transfers of the debtor's property.

Balance Sheet—This refers to a statement of financial conditions as of a specific date. It is different from a cash flow statement, which summarizes income and expenses.

Bankruptcy Code—The legal instrument filed with the bankruptcy court that commences a bankruptcy proceeding.

Bankruptcy Petition—The legal instrument filed with the bankruptcy court that commences a bankruptcy proceeding.

Bar Date—This is the last date for filing a proof of claim.

Beneficiary—This refers to someone who receives benefits or funds under a will or other contract, such as an insurance policy.

Beneficiary Transfer—When one names a beneficiary in an insurance policy or in an employee benefit plan and the proceeds pay out to the beneficiary, the result is a beneficiary transfer.

Bequest—This means to leave (bequeath) personal property to another by Last Will and Testament.

Bypass Trust—A trust which contains property on which Federal Taxes are paid at the death of the first spouse to die, and which typically is not taxed at the second death. Where the optimum marital deduction plan is used, the tax on the property in this trust is paid by the Applicable Credit Amount and it is sometimes referred to as the Credit Shelter Trust.

Call Risk—This refers to the possibility that falling interest rates will cause a bond issuer to redeem—or call—its high-yielding bond before the bond's maturity date.

Chapter 7—In a Chapter 7 proceeding, the debtor's business is liquidated, and its assets are distributed to creditors with allowed proofs of claim.

Chapter 11—Normally, a Chapter 11 proceeding is a reorganization proceeding. The debtor continues to operate its business after the bankruptcy is filed. Chapter 11 liquidators are not uncommon and usually are the result of an unsuccessful reorganization attempt.

Closing—When a bankruptcy case is closed, it is no longer in the court's docket.

Codicil—To make an addition to a will, or to change, explain, revoke, or add provisions.

Co-Trustee—Whenever there are two or more concurrent trustees of a trust, they are called Co-Trustees.

Collateral—This refers to the property of a debtor in which a creditor has a lien securing its debt.

Community Property—Ten states (Alaska, Arizona, California, Idaho, Louisiana, Nevada, New Mexico, Texas, Washington, and Wisconsin) use some form of the community property system to determine the interest of a husband and wife in property acquired during marriage.

Complaint—A pleading that is filed to initiate a lawsuit or an adversary proceeding.

Composition—Out of court agreement to pay a percentage of a debt in full settlement.

Conversion—The conversion of a bankruptcy case from one chapter type to another.

Corporate Trustee—If an individual is the trustee of his or her own trust that individual is an individual trustee. When a bank, or trust company is named as the trustee it is known as a Corporate Trustee.

Country Risk—The possibility that political events (a war, national elections), financial problems (rising inflation, government default), or natural disasters (an earthquake, a poor harvest) will weaken a country's economy and cause investments in that country to decline.

Credit Risk—This refers to the possibility that a bond issuer will fail to repay interest and principal in a timely manner. Also called default risk.

Credit Shelter Trust— The Credit Shelter Trust allows each spouse to pass on an estate worth up to $2,000,000.00 without incurring any transfer taxes. This is called the "applicable exclusion amount." However, beginning in 2011, that amount drops to $1,000,000.

Crummey Trust—An irrevocable life insurance trust that has "Crummey Powers" incorporated into the document. The "Crummey Power" allows one to make a gift of up to $10,000 per donee, per year, (although usually less than this amount) into the trust. The current income beneficiary(s) has the right to withdraw the gifted amount during a specified period. If the withdrawal does not take place, the gift amount defaults to the trust, and remains in the trust to pay insurance premiums.

Currency Risk—The possibility that returns could be reduced for Americans investing in foreign securities because of a rise in the value of the U.S. dollar against foreign currencies.

Debtor—One who owes debts. In bankruptcy, the bankrupt business that is under the control and protection of the bankruptcy court is the debtor.

Debtor-In Possession (DIP)—The business debtor in a Chapter 11 reorganization. In a Chapter 11, the debtor retaining possession of the assets involved in the bankruptcy.

Decedent—The person who has died.

Devise—To leave property by will. Historically a "devise" only referred to a transfer of real property, not personal property, but Utah law now uses the term for both forms of property.

Discharge—A discharge in bankruptcy relieves the debtor of the dischargeable debts incurred prior to filing. Discharge is the legal term for the elimination of debt through bankruptcy.

Dismissal—The dismissal of a bankruptcy case, for all intents and purposes, returns the debtor to the same place it was before bankruptcy was filed.

DOD—A common abbreviation for "Date of Death."

Durable Power of Attorney—A written legal document that lets an individual designate another person to act on his or her behalf, even in the event the individual becomes disabled or incapacitated.

Durable Power of Attorney for Health Care—A written legal document that gives another person the authority to act on one's behalf regarding health care decisions.

Elective Share—The Elective Share is the share of a Decedent's assets which the surviving spouse can elect to receive, under the State probate code regardless of the provisions of the Decedent's Will or Trust. This share was formerly known as the "Dower" right and was equal to the amount the spouse would have received under the intestate succession statute if there had been no Will. The modern Elective Share was instituted under the Uniform Probate Code, which has been adopted by many states in the United States

Estate—The property or assets that an individual owns or has rights to.

Estate Plan—The overall plan devised by the estate planning professional with the help of the grantor, to pass the estate of the grantor on to the remainder beneficiaries. This plan usually includes wills, trusts, right to die documents, limited partnerships, limited liability companies, and related documents as drafted by the attorney. There may also be provisions on how to manage the assets of the grantors while they are still alive and capable, or if they should become incapacitated.

Estate Tax—A tax imposed at one's death on the transfer of most types of property.

Examiner—An officer of the court is sometimes appointed to investigate the financial affairs of the debtor.

Executor—The person named in a will to manage an estate. This person will collect the property, pay any debt, and distribute the property or assets according to the will.

Exemption or Exempt Property—Property of an individual debtor that the law protects from the actions of creditors, such as the debtor's residence or homestead, automobile, and the like.

Fiduciary—A person or institution legally responsible for the management, investment, and distributions of funds

Foreclosure—A debt-collection whereby property of the debtor is sold on the courthouse steps to satisfy debts. Foreclosure often involves real estate of the debtor.

Funding—The act of transferring the title to assets into the name of the trustee from the name of the grantor.

Generation Skipping Tax—This tax, instituted in 1984, taxes the transfer of wealth from the decedent to generations more remote than his or her children. Each person has an exemption of $1,030,000 from this tax(as indexed for inflation.) Once more that this amount has been left to a grandchild or great-grandchild, etc., a tax is imposed on the transfer at a flat 55% rate. The advent of this tax has curtailed the use of the "Generation Skipping Trust", so that such trusts now are usually the recipient of only the exempt amount, to be held for the benefit of remote beneficiaries.

Gift—A gratuitous transfer of property to someone else, without receiving adequate consideration in return.

Gift Program—Usually a planned program of making annual gifts to beneficiaries within the amount of the Annual Exclusion.

Grantor—The person who transfers assets into a trust for the benefit of another.

Gross Estate—The total property or assets held by an individual as defined for federal estate tax purposes.

Gross-up Gift taxes—If gifts have been made within three years of the year of death on which gift taxes were actually paid, those gift taxes will be added back to the value of the estate for purposes of computing the estate tax. This is called gift tax gross-up.

Guardian—The person legally entrusted with the care of a minor child.

Heir—A person who is to receive assets under the laws of intestacy in the absence of a will. In common usage, however, the term is inaccurately applied to a person who receives benefits as a beneficiary under the terms of a will.

Incapacity—The lack of ability to act on one's own behalf.

Income—Normally, the trust or will designates what income is and what is principal. In the absence of designation language, there is a "Uniform Principal and Income Act" under the "Uniform Probate Code" which would outline what is income and what is principal. If one lives in a" Non-Uniform Probate Code" state, then state statute will govern what to designate as income and principal in the absence of governing language in the document.

Income Beneficiary—The person who will receive the income from a trust for a specified period of time (e.g., "beneficiary for life").

Income Risk—The possibility that the dividends paid by a fixed-income investment, such as a bond, will decline because of falling overall interest rates.

Industry Risk—The possibility that a group of stocks in a single industry will decline in price due to developments in that industry.

Inflation Risk—The possibility that increases in the cost of living will reduce or eliminate an investment's real (inflation-adjusted) returns.

Inheritance Tax—Technically, a death tax which is levied by a State upon each taker of a decedents' property, as opposed to an estate tax which is levied on the estate as a whole.

Interest Rate Risk—The possibility that a bond investment will decline in value because of an increase in interest rates.

Inter vivos—A type of trust created during one's lifetime to hold property for the benefit of another.

Intestacy, Intestate—The term applied when an individual dies without a will.

Irrevocable—Indicating something that cannot be changed or terminated.

Joint Property – This is property where title is held in Joint Tenancy so that the surviving co-owner[s] own the entire asset by operation of law at the death of any owner. In a marriage, this property usually qualifies as marital property for marital deduction purposes

Joint Tenancy with Right of Survivorship—A title that can be placed on property that is co-owned. At the death of one of the co-owners, the other will become the sole owner of the property, regardless of what may be conveyed in the will.

Lien—An interest in property securing the repayment of a debt.

Life Insurance Gift Value—The value of a life insurance policy which is given to someone else. Normally, this value is very close to the cash surrender value. In most cases the gift value will be less than the face value of the policy. Where the insured is in bad health, and could not obtain new insurance within normal cost limits, the gift value of the policy may be greater than the face value.

Living Trust—A revocable trust established by a grantor during his or her lifetime in which the grantor transfers some or all of his or her property into the trust.

Living Will—A legal document directing that the maker's or signer's life is not to be artificially supported in the event of a terminal illness or accident.

Lump Sum Gift—Typically, a gift which is made on a one-time basis only, as opposed to a gift program, which is designed to use the annual exclusion on a yearly basis.

Manager Risk—The possibility that an actively managed stock or bond fund's investment adviser will fail to execute the fund's investment strategy effectively and, as a result, the fund will fail to achieve its stated objective.

Marital Deduction—A deduction allowing for the unlimited transfer of any or all property from one spouse to the other generally free of estate and gift tax.

Marital Property—In general usage, property acquired by a married couple during the marriage from their separate or joint efforts including wages, profits, etc. Marital Property is similar to what would be community property if the couple had resided in a community property state. Marital Property does not include gifts, inheritances or assets acquired prior to marriage.

Minor Child—A minor child is a person who has not yet reached the legal age of majority. This age can differ with each state, but generally is between 16 and 18 years. The term does not apply to an emancipated youth.

Marginal Estate Tax Rate—The tax rate at which the top dollars in an estate are taxed.

Market Risk—The possibility that stock or bond prices overall will decline over short or even extended periods. Stock and bond markets tend to move in cycles, with periods when prices rise and other periods when prices fall.

Motion—A request for the court to act. A motion may be filed within a lawsuit, adversary proceeding, or bankruptcy case.

Per Stirpes—A term used in a will or trust which designates that property will pass to descendants "by branches" so that a Decedent's children divide equally the same share the Decedent would have taken at each level of descent.

Personal Property—Property that is not permanently attached to land.

Personal Representative—The person who manages the assets of an estate, using the will, if any, as a guide, through the probate process. This person was formerly known as the Executor or Executrix.

Petition for Relief—The papers filed initiating a bankruptcy case.

Possessory Security Interest—A security interest or lien on property that requires the creditor to have possession of the property, such as a pawn or pledge.

Power of Appointment—A right given to another in a written instrument, such as a will or trust, that allows the other to decide how to distribute property. The power of appointment is "general" if it places no restrictions on who the distributees may be. A power is "limited" or "special" if it limits the eventual distributee.

Power of Attorney—Power of Attorney is a written legal document that gives an individual the authority to act for another.

Preference—A transfer of property of the debtor to a creditor made immediately prior to the debtor's bankruptcy that enables the creditor to receive more than it would have received from the bankruptcy. A preferential transfer must be made while the debtor was insolvent and as payment for a debt that existed prior to the transfer of property.

Principal Risk—The possibility that an investment will go down in value, or "lose money."

Probate—The review or testing of a will before a court of law to ensure that it is authentic.

Representative—Someone who is authorized to act on one's behalf, such as an executor or a trustee.

State Death or Inheritance Taxes—The tax imposed by the state in which an individual lives and/or where the property is located, if different, on the transfer of that property to another at one's death.

Successor Trustee—The person designated in the document or named later who assumes the duties of trustee after the death, incapacity, or resignation of the original trustee.

Survivor—Usually referring to the surviving spouse in a marriage.

Testamentary Trust—A trust that is created upon an individual's death by the terms of the will.

Testator/Testatrix—A person who makes a will.

Trust—A written legal instrument created by a grantor during his or her lifetime or at death for the benefit of another.

Trustee—This is the person named in a trust document who will manage the property owned by the trust and distribute any income according to the document. A trustee can be an individual or a corporate fiduciary.

Will—A formal testamentary document which outlines the wishes of the Testator or maker of the will. This document will normally outline who the beneficiaries are, and what assets are to be distributed to them. It will also name a "Personal Representative" (formerly known as an Executor) to manage the assets through the probate process.

Witness—A term used to describe those who attest to the validity of a will or trust. A will must be witnessed to be valid in most states. Witnesses should not have a beneficial interest in the will, and should be of sound mind and legal age

Don't miss out!

Visit the website below and you can sign up to receive emails whenever Sharon O'Maley publishes a new book. There's no charge and no obligation.

https://books2read.com/r/B-A-NVXZ-MFWNC

BOOKS 2 READ

Connecting independent readers to independent writers.

About the Author

Sharon Finch O'Maley was born in Xenia, Ohio to a preacher and his wife, Ralph and Ruth Finch. She moved with her parents and older sister, Marilyn, to Indiana, New Jersey, Colorado, and back to Ohio and to Nebraska through her childhood. She graduated from college with a degree in Elementary Education. She taught school for the following seven years.

Her dream of being a missionary in a Spanish-speaking country came true in 1982 when she went to Costa Rica for five months. In 1986, she was assigned to go to the Dominican Republic for three years. Many of the stories in "At the Break Of Dawn" are her experiences with the people she loved so much.

Sharon is presently living in Austin, Texas and is the mother of a daughter, Ruth who attended University of Texas in Austin, Texas and is now married to her high school sweetheart, Steve Largaespada and has two young sons.

Sharon has been published in various magazines, newspapers, and daily devotional books. She is a daily blogger on Dr. Strains CBD.

www.ingramcontent.com/pod-product-compliance
Lightning Source LLC
LaVergne TN
LVHW090430210926
848480LV00002B/771